$23.60

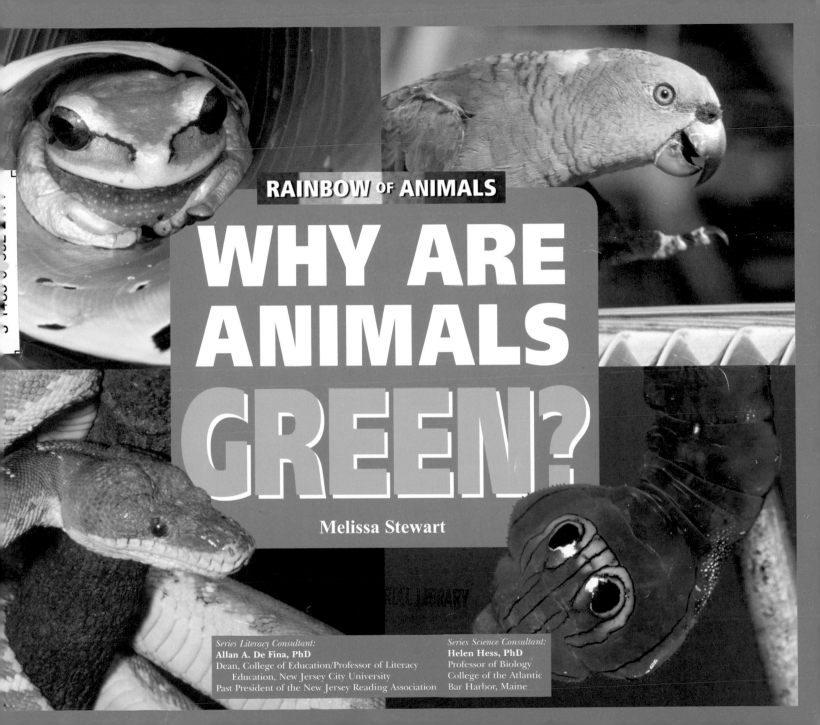

RAINBOW OF ANIMALS

WHY ARE ANIMALS GREEN?

Melissa Stewart

Series Literacy Consultant:
Allan A. De Fina, PhD
Dean, College of Education/Professor of Literacy
    Education, New Jersey City University
Past President of the New Jersey Reading Association

Series Science Consultant:
Helen Hess, PhD
Professor of Biology
College of the Atlantic
Bar Harbor, Maine

Contents

Words to Know

algae (AL jee)—Plant-like creatures that use sunlight, water, and a gas called carbon dioxide to make food.

attract (uh TRAKT)—To make interested.

blend in—To match; to look the same as.

predator (PREH duh tur)—An animal that hunts and kills other animals for food.

survive (sur VYV)—To stay alive.

tropical (TRAH pih cuhl) rain forest—A warm forest with at least 100 inches of rain a year. The forest is green all year.

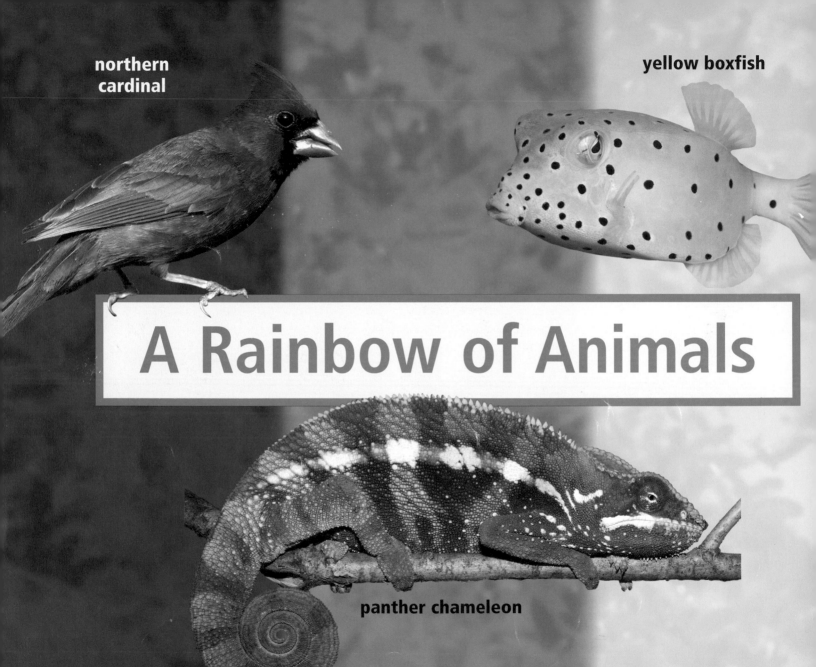

northern
cardinal

yellow boxfish

A Rainbow of Animals

panther chameleon

poison dart
frog

Go outside and look around. How many kinds of animals do you see? Fish and frogs are animals. So are birds and insects. Animals come in all sizes and shapes. And they come in all the colors of the rainbow.

leaf-mimic katydid

lesser purple
emperor butterfly

Green Animals Near You

Can you think of some green animals that live near you? Many frogs are green. So are some insects.

Green animals live in other parts of the world too. Let's take a look at some of them.

8

Leaf-Mimic Katydid

Small animals have many enemies. Their body colors often help them stay safe.

This little green insect looks like a leaf. Its shape and color help it blend in with its forest home.

Green Spider

This young spider does not live in the forest. It lives in a grassy field. But its shape and color still help this spider hide from **predators**.

Masked Puddle Frog

Animals cannot watch for danger when they are asleep. When this little frog feels tired, it curls up inside a leaf. The frog's green skin matches the leaf. That helps it stay safe while it takes a nap.

Yellow-Crowned Parrot

This parrot lives in **tropical rain forests**. Its green feathers make it hard to spot. When two of these birds need to find each other, they make loud calls. Then they fly toward the sound.

Green Anole Lizard

Most of the time, this lizard stays green. That helps it blend in with its forest home. But when an anole is worried or angry, it turns brown. The color change sends a message. It tells other lizards to stay away.

Green Sea Turtle

There are many green animals on land. Some live in the ocean too.

A green sea turtle spends most of its time eating sea grass. It is hard to spot as it glides through the water. That helps it stay safe from sharks and other enemies.

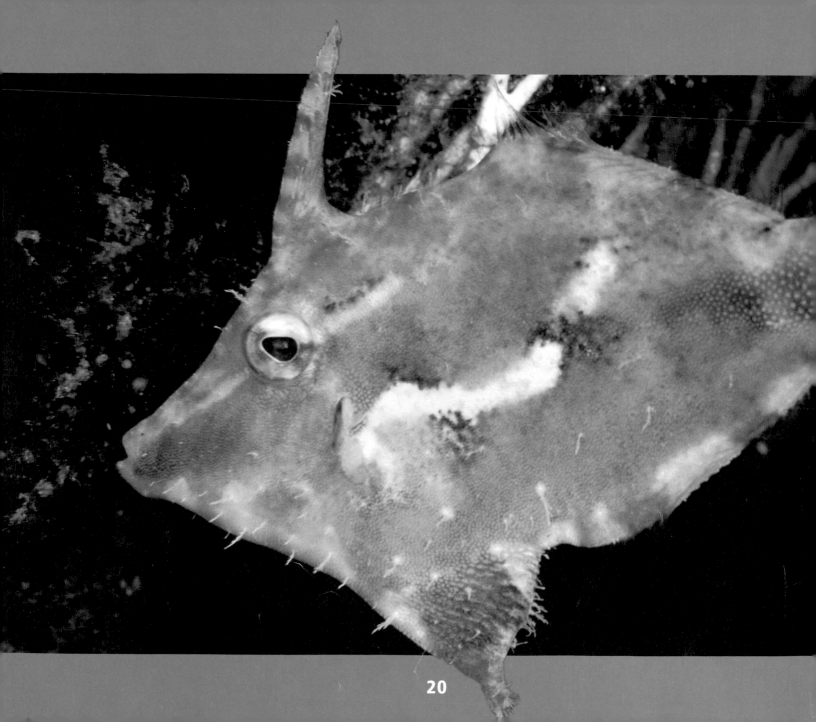

Diamond Leatherjacket Fish

This fish has a trick for staying safe. Its body looks just like the green **algae** it swims through all day long. When hungry predators pass by, they do not notice the little fish. It blends in with its home.

Brown-Throated Three-Toed Sloth

Algae often grow on a sloth's shaggy fur. During the day, these animals hang from trees and sleep. The green algae help the sloths blend in with their forest home, so hungry wild cats cannot spot them.

Mallard Duck

Sometimes being green helps an animal stand out. A male mallard's green head is easy to see. It helps him **attract** a mate. A female mallard has a brown head. It helps her hide from enemies while she sits on her eggs.

Costa Rican leaf moth caterpillar

Guessing Game

Being green helps many kinds of animals survive in the world. It helps some animals hide from enemies. It helps others stand out so they can find mates. How do you think being green helps the animals in these photos?

(See answers on page 32.)

emerald tree boa

Where Do These Green

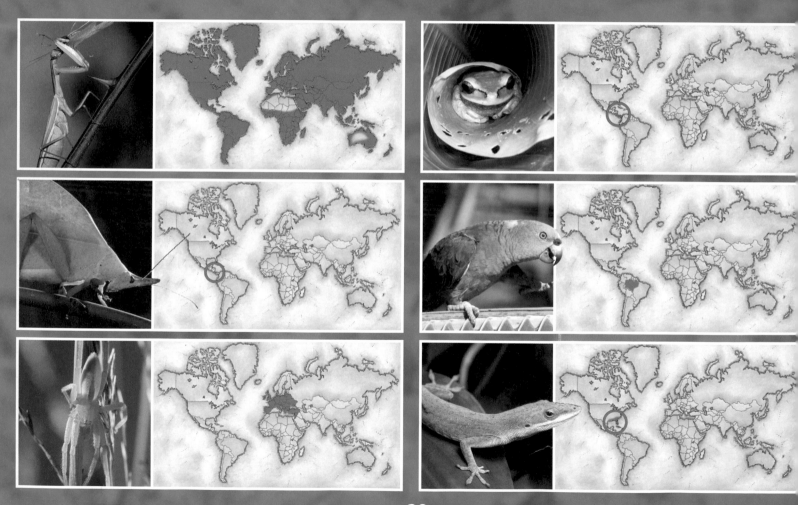

Animals Live?

KEY:
The orange areas on each map below show where that animal lives.

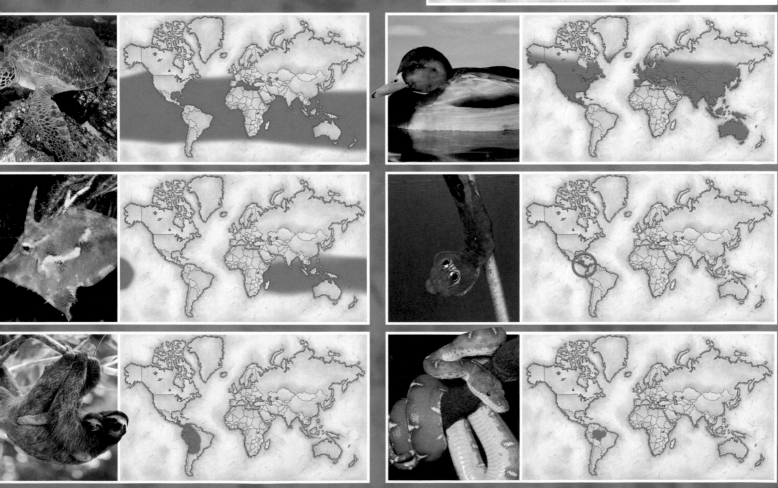

Learn More

Books

Arnosky, Jim. *I See Animals Hiding*. New York: Scholastic, 2000.

Jenkins, Steve. *Living Color*. Boston: Houghton Mifflin, 2007.

Kalman, Bobbie, and John Crossingham. *Camouflage: Changing to Hide*. New York: Crabtree Publishing, 2005.

Stockland, Patricia. *Red Eyes or Blue Feathers: A Book About Animal Colors*. Minneapolis: Picture Window Books, 2005.

Whitehouse, Patricia. *Colors We Eat: Green Foods*. Chicago: Heinemann, 2004.

Learn More

Web Sites

Animal Colors

http://www.highlightskids.com/Science/Stories/SS1000_
animalColors.asp

Beasts Playground: Camouflage Game

http://www.abc.net.au/beasts/playground/camouflage.htm

How Animal Camouflage Works

http://science.howstuffworks.com/animal-camouflage1.htm

Index

Enslow Elementary, an imprint of Enslow Publishers, Inc.

Enslow Elementary® is a registered trademark of Enslow Publishers, Inc.

Copyright © 2009 by Melissa Stewart

All rights reserved.

No part of this book may be reproduced by any means without the written permission of the publisher.

Library of Congress Cataloging-in-Publication Data

Stewart, Melissa.
    Why are animals green? / Melissa Stewart.
        p. cm. — (Rainbow of animals)
    Includes bibliographical references.
    Summary: "Uses examples of animals in the wild to explain why some animals are green"—Provided by publisher.
    ISBN: 978-0-7660-3252-1
    1. Animals—Color—Juvenile literature. 2. Green—Juvenile literature. I. Title.
    QL767.S746 2009
    591.47'2—dc22   2008011470

ISBN-10: 0-7660-3252-3

Printed in the United States of America

10 9 8 7 6 5 4 3 2 1

All photos by Minden Pictures:
Interior: © Barry Mansell/npl, p. 5 (frog); © Birgitte Wilms, pp. 20–21, 29 (fish); © Chri Newbert, p. 4 (boxfish); © Cisca Castelijns/Foto Natura, pp. 6–7, 28 (mantis); © Frans Lanting pp. 5 (katydid), 8–9, 24–25, 28 (katydid), 29 (duck); © Fred Bavendam, pp. 18–19, 29 (turtle © Gerry Ellis, pp. 1 (bottom left), 16–17, 27, 28 (lizard), 29 (snake); © Hans Cristoph Kappel/np p. 5 (butterfly); © Ingo Arndt/Foto Natura, pp. 1 (bottom right), 26, 29 (caterpillar); © Konra Wothe, pp. 1 (top right), 14–15, 28 (parrot); © Michael & Patricia Fogden, pp. 1 (top left), 12–1 22–23, 28 (frog), 29 (sloth); © Pete Oxford, p. 4 (chameleon); © Stephen Dalton, pp. 10–11, 2 (spider); © Tom Vezo, p. 4 (cardinal).
Cover: (clockwise from top left) © Michael & Patricia Fogden; © Konrad Wothe; © Ing Arndt/Foto Natura; © Gerry Ellis.

Illustration Credits: © 1999, Artville, LLC, pp. 28–29 (maps).

Note to Parents and Teachers: The *Rainbow of Animals* series supports the National Scienc Education Standards for K–4 science. The Words to Know section introduces subject-specifi vocabulary words, including pronunciation and definitions. Early readers may need help wit these new words.

Answers to the Guessing Game:

The green body of the Costa Rican leaf moth caterpillar matches the plants on which it lives. That makes it hard to spot.

The emerald tree boa's colors help it hide from enemies. The colors also help this snake sneak up on animals to eat.

Enslow Elementary
an imprint of
E | **Enslow Publishers, Inc.**
40 Industrial Road
Box 398
Berkeley Heights, NJ 07922
USA
http://www.enslow.com